learn to draw
Dogs & Puppies

Learn to draw and color 25 favorite
dog breeds, step by easy step,
shape by simple shape!

Illustrated by Diana Fisher

Getting Started

When you look closely at the drawings in this book, you'll notice that they're made up of basic shapes, such as circles, triangles, and rectangles. To draw all your favorite dogs and puppies, just start with simple shapes as you see here. It's easy and fun!

Circles are used to draw this dog's head, chest, and hips.

Ovals are good for drawing a sitting dog's chest and hips.

Squares are best for drawing a dog that has a blocky head.

Coloring Tips

There's more than one way to bring your furry friends to life on paper—you can use crayons, markers, or colored pencils. Just be sure you have plenty of good "dog colors"— black, brown, and white, plus yellow, orange, and red.

Pencil

Colored pencil

Crayon

Marker

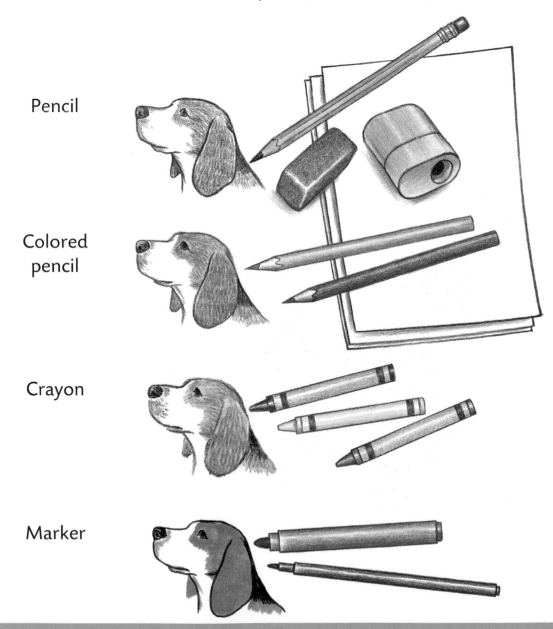

Pug Puppy

Adult Pugs have square faces with deep wrinkles. But this Pug is just a pup, so its face is smoother and more rounded.

1

2

3

4

6

5

Chihuahua

Use circles for the chihuahua's tiny body.
Then draw short legs. Be sure to add big,
round eyes and large, triangular ears!

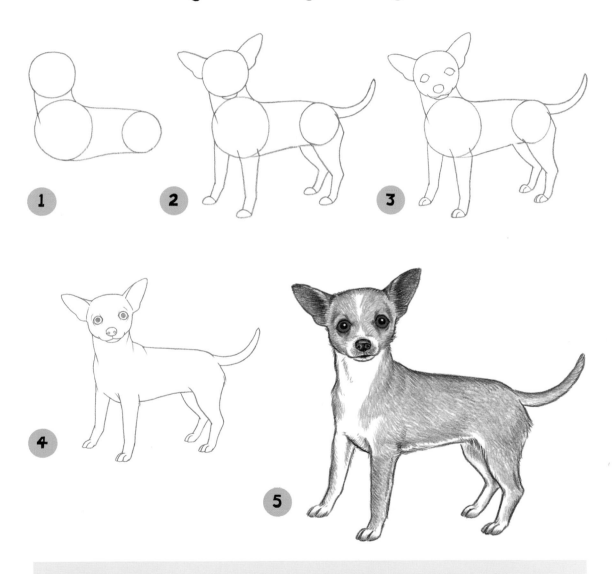

fun fact According to the American Kennel Club (AKC), the Chihuahua is the smallest breed of dog! A full-grown Chihuahua measures from 6 to 9 inches tall at the shoulder and weighs only 2 to 6 pounds!

Great Dane

This gentle giant is very tall with a long body. Draw a big circle for the chest. Then add the head and hips with smaller circles.

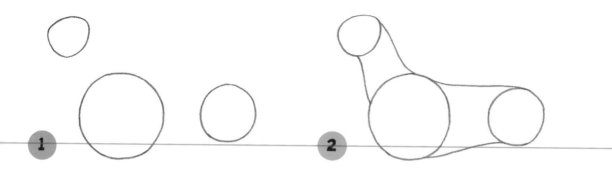

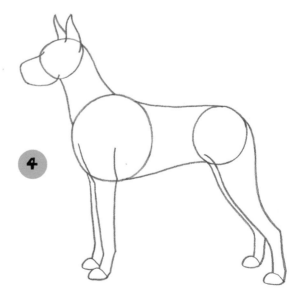

fun fact

The name "Great Dane" makes people think these dogs are Danish (from Denmark). But the Great Dane (also known as Deutsche Dogge, meaning "German Dog") is the national dog of Germany, where the breed originated.

The dog shown here is brindle colored. But Great Danes can also be black, blue, fawn, or harlequin.

5

6

7

Beagle

When drawing this popular hound,
look at its unique features, such as its straight
forelegs, upright tail, and long ears.

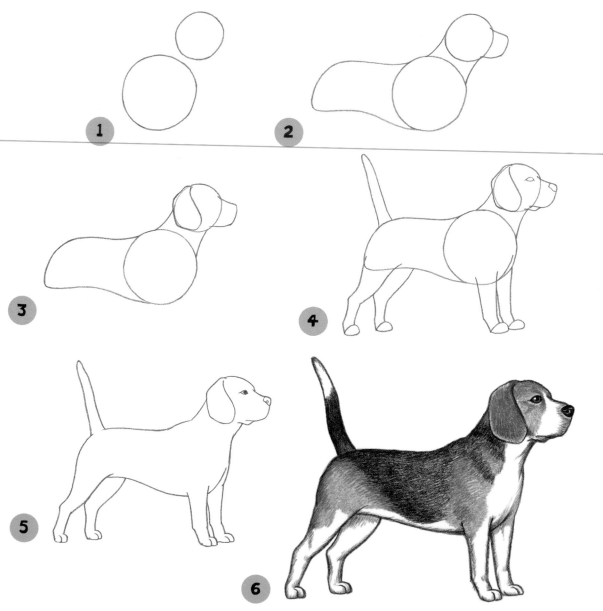

Scottish Terrier

scottie dogs have many unusual features, including a long head, ears that stand up straight, a bushy beard, and "eyebrow" tufts.

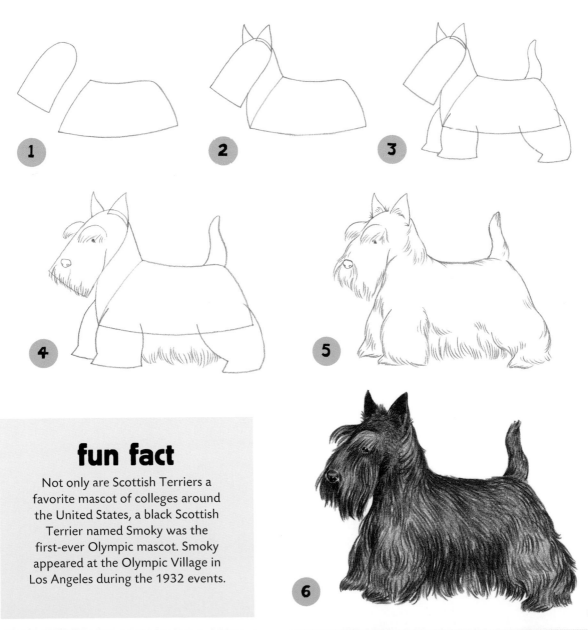

fun fact

Not only are Scottish Terriers a favorite mascot of colleges around the United States, a black Scottish Terrier named Smoky was the first-ever Olympic mascot. Smoky appeared at the Olympic Village in Los Angeles during the 1932 events.

Old English Sheepdog Puppy

A shaggy Sheepdog might look like
just a big, cuddly ball of fur, but underneath
all that hair is a strong body.

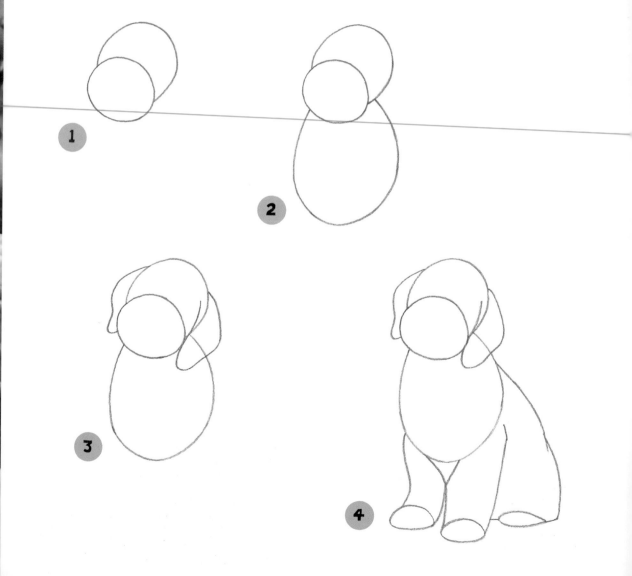

5

6

7

Airedale Terrier

This bearded breed has a flat, deep chest, so start by drawing an oval for the body. Then add a rectangle for the head.

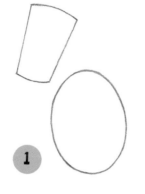

1

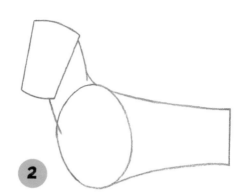

2

3

4

5

6

Pomeranian

The Pom's body is very round, making this small pup look like a circular bundle of fur with tiny legs!

Parson Russell Terrier Puppy

These lovable pups are white with patches of black
or tan. Their bright eyes are large and round,
and their ears fold forward.

fun fact

In 2003, the Jack Russell Terrier
became the Parson Russell Terrier.
This breed was named after the
Reverend John ("Jack") Russell.
Nicknamed "the hunting parson,"
the reverend developed the
breed to run long distances with
Foxhounds.

1

2

3

4

5

Golden Retriever Puppy

Best known for the color of their coats,
Goldens also have strong legs, round paws,
and large, wide-set eyes.

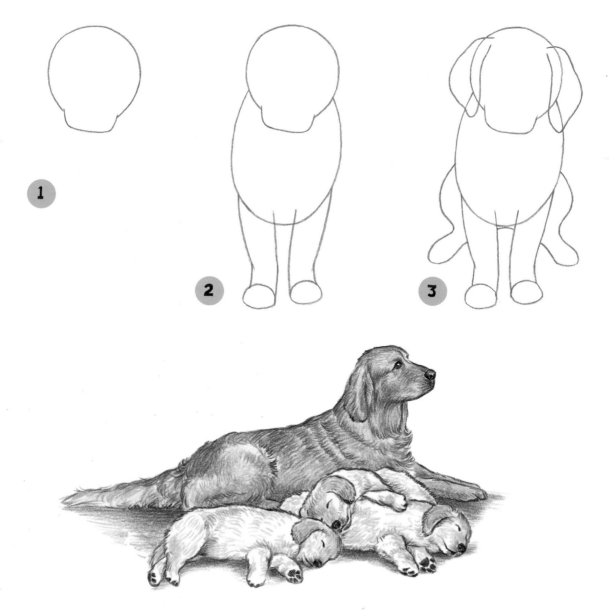

Since the Golden Retriever was developed in England and Scotland in the 1800s, it has had many names. Until 1920, the breed was known as the Golden Flat-Coat. They've also been called "Yellow Retrievers" and "Russian Retrievers."

The rich, golden coat of this retriever comes in various shades—from light to dark.

4

5

6

Bouvier des Flandres

This shaggy herding dog has a rough coat, a thick beard, and a "fall" of hair that covers its eyes.

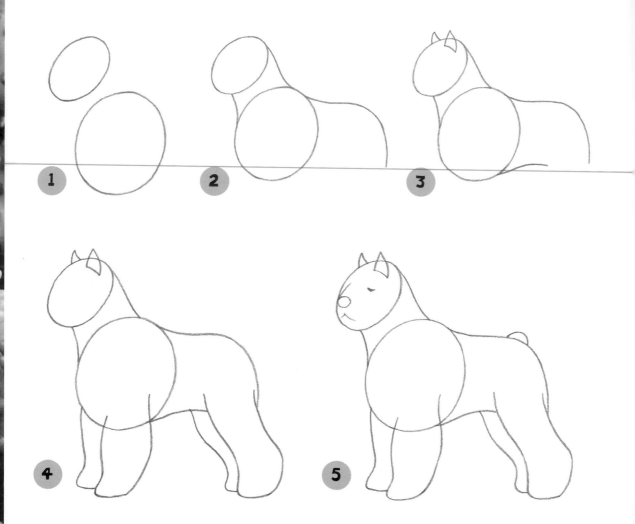

6

7

Often black or gray, Bouviers can also be fawn, brindled, or salt-and-pepper colored.

8

Dogs in Action

From performing in championship shows to working with human companions, these canines do it all! Why not try drawing these active dogs?

Agility contests are like dog Olympics—here a Pomeranian shows its ability to follow commands and handle an A-frame obstacle.

German Shepherd Dogs often get special training to become seeing-eye dogs who safely lead the blind.

Some dogs are trained to go on rescue missions. Saint Bernards are used to find lost travelers in the Swiss Alps.

Herding breeds, such as the Old English Sheepdog, work
to control the movement of livestock, including sheep,
cattle, deer, and even chickens!

Other "working dogs" have learned to pull sleds or carts. For example, Bouviers
were originally bred as farm dogs who both herded cattle and pulled milk carts.
Today's Bouvs still enjoy carting exercises!

English Springer Spaniel

The lively Springer is a hunting dog with long ears, a round head, and a rectangular muzzle.

Dachshund

These low-to-the-ground pooches have long, thin bodies with a sausage shape, earning them the nickname "wiener dogs"!

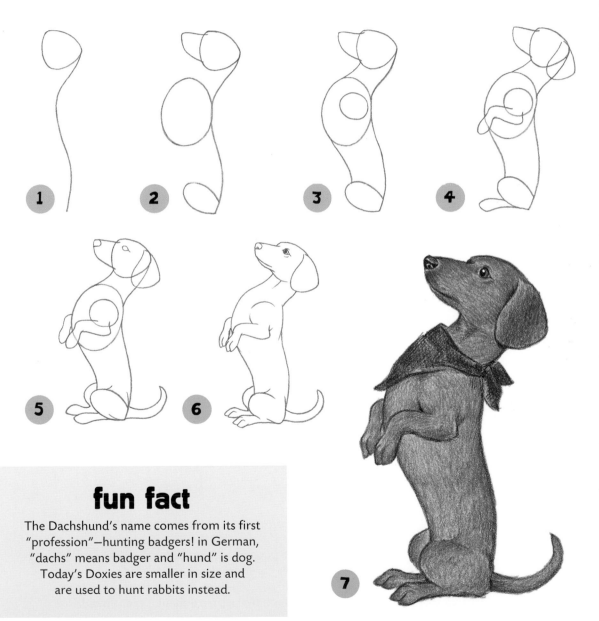

fun fact

The Dachshund's name comes from its first "profession"—hunting badgers! in German, "dachs" means badger and "hund" is dog. Today's Doxies are smaller in size and are used to hunt rabbits instead.

Dalmatian Puppy

It's easy to spot a Dalmatian! Dals have round markings, round hips, and rounded ears.

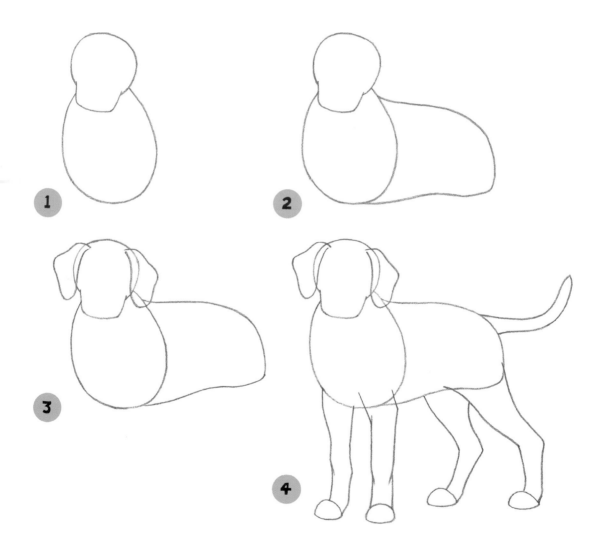

fun fact

Dalmatian puppies are born with solid white coats! When they are between 2 and 6 weeks old, they begin to develop spots. The spots continue to grow until the pups are about 6 months old.

5

6

7

Siberian Husky

The Husky is a sled dog with an athletic body. Draw an oval to create this dog's deep chest— and don't forget its bushy tail!

fun fact

Siberian Huskies are known for their striking eye colors, which range from sky blue to reddish amber.
It is not uncommon for a Husky to have two eyes of different colors (called "bi-eyed") or for a Husky to have one eye of two different colors (called "parti-eyed").

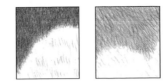

In addition to the black and white shown here, a Husky's coat can be gray and white, red and white, or solid white.

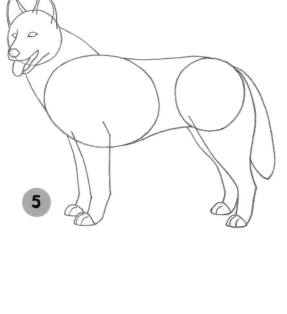

5

6

7

Papillon

In French, papillon means "butterfly."
These dogs were named for their large,
fringed ears that resemble butterfly wings!

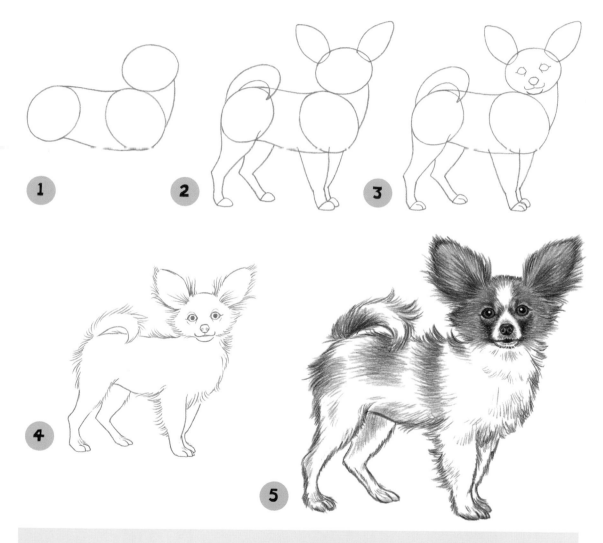

fun fact

In the 1600s, Papillons were known as Dwarf Spaniels, and they had "drop ears" that hung down. The breed was renamed when puppies began appearing with large, pricked ears. Today's Papillons may have either ear type.

Puli

with their long cords of hair that look
like dreadlocks, Pulis mop up attention!
The cords are shorter on their heads.

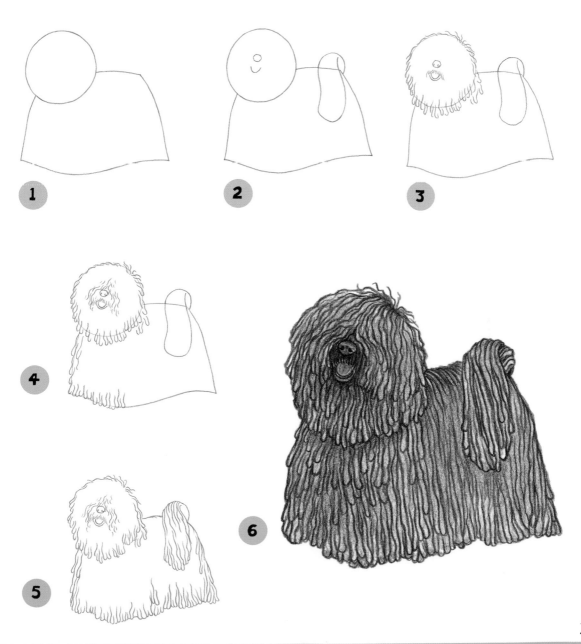

German Shepherd

This popular breed has a long, strong body.
Be sure to draw large, athletic thighs on
this proud, powerful canine—and make its muzzle
about half the length of its head.

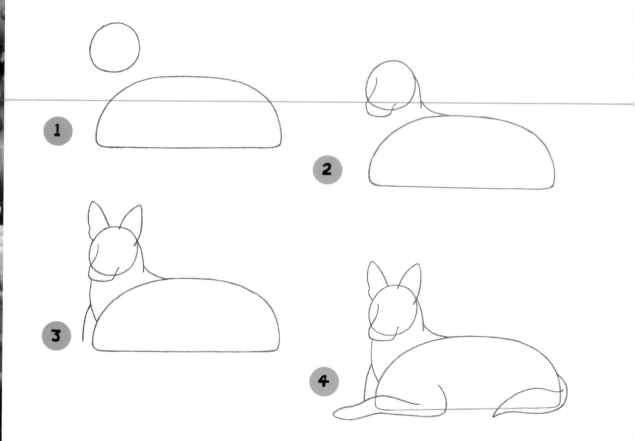

fun fact

German Shepherds are often used as guard dogs, police dogs, and military dogs. Intelligent and hard working, these canines also help detect drugs and bombs, perform search-and-rescue missions, and track missing persons.

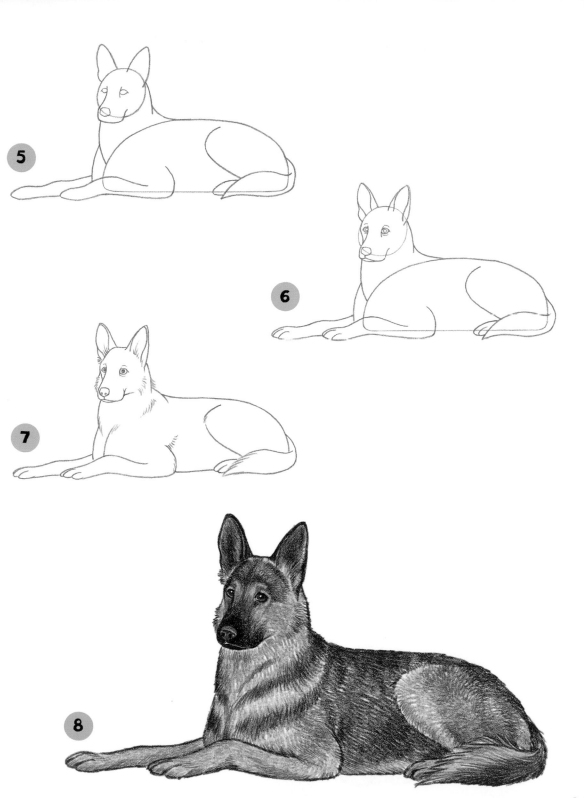

Basset Hound Puppy

The Basset is well loved for its wrinkles, sagging jowls, and long ears.

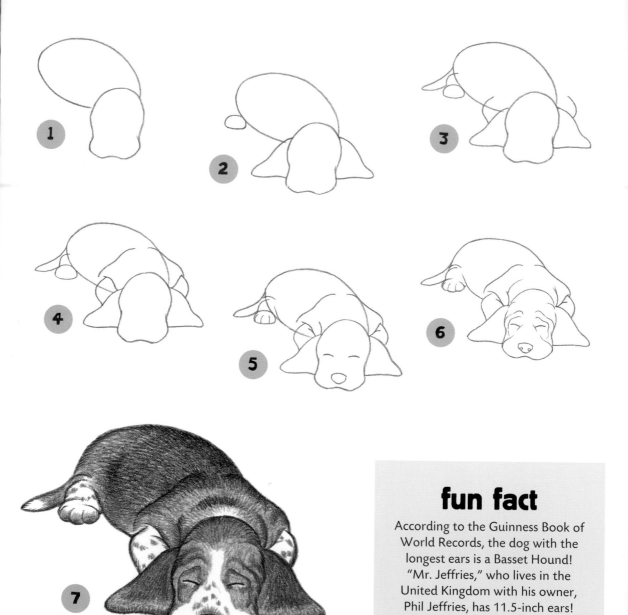

fun fact

According to the Guinness Book of World Records, the dog with the longest ears is a Basset Hound! "Mr. Jeffries," who lives in the United Kingdom with his owner, Phil Jeffries, has 11.5-inch ears!

Great Pyrenees

The Great Pyrenees has a lamb's character but a lion's look! This giant dog's face is framed by small, flat ears and a mane of hair.

Standard Poodle

The traditional Poodle cut—which includes pompoms—shows off the Standard Poodle's pointed muzzle and muscular hind legs.

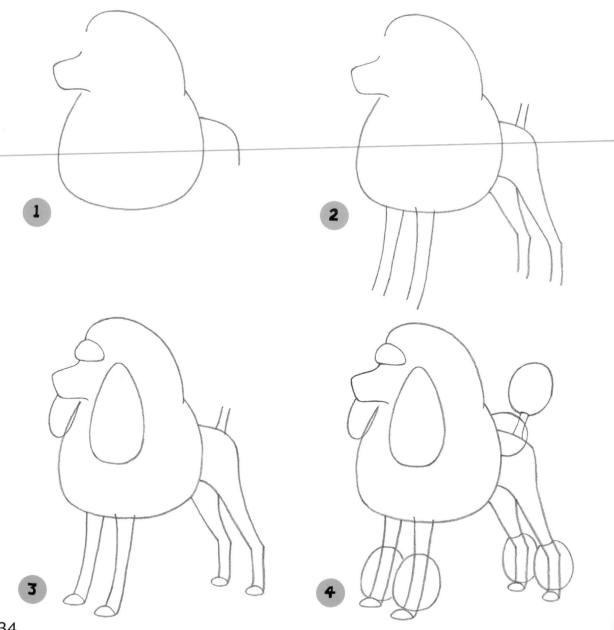

5

6

7

fun fact

Many people call the Standard Poodle a "French Poodle" because of its history as a show dog and circus dog in France. But this breed actually originated in Germany. Bred as a duck retriever, the Poodle's name comes from the German word "pudelin," which means "to splash in water." The Standard Poodle's traditional haircut makes it easier for the dog to swim; the pompoms of fur keep the dog's joints warm.

Italian Greyhound

Although this miniature version of the
Greyhound has a thin and fragile look,
the breed is actually very strong and sturdy.

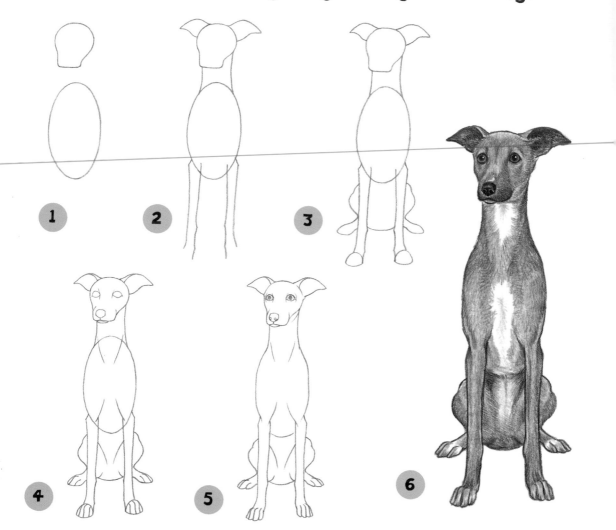

fun fact

Italian Greyhounds were a favorite pet of
ancient Egyptians. Mummies of these lovable dogs
have been found in the tombs of Egypt.

Akita Puppy

A native of Japan, the Akita has a
thick body; a tail that curls forward; ears that
stand up straight; and large, wide paws.

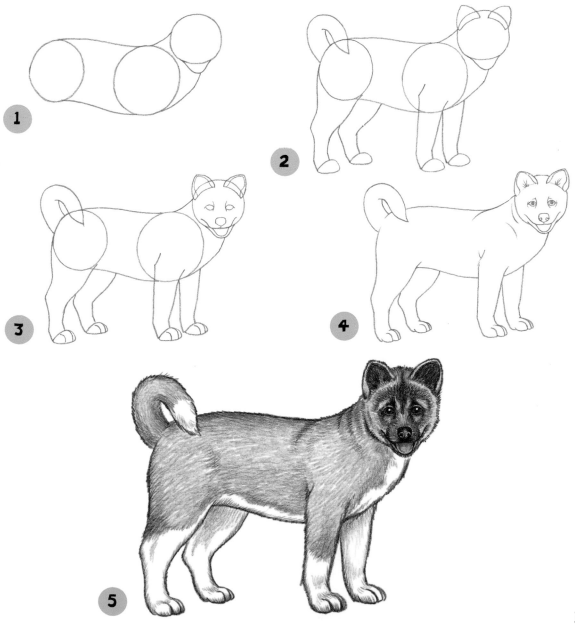

Rough Collie

The Rough collie's mane is eye-catching because it is so full and bushy—much like the breed's long, fluffy tail. But the feature the collie is best known for is its intelligent expression!

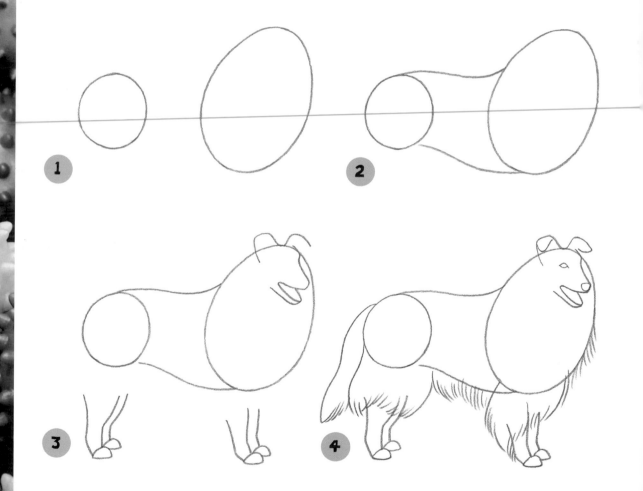

fun fact

Originally a sheep-herding dog in Scotland, the rough collie developed a thick, fluffy coat to keep it warm during the cold and harsh weather.

5

6

7

The Collie shown here
is sable and white.
They can also be white,
tricolor, or blue merle.

Australian Shepherd Puppies

The thick ruff of fur on an Australian Shepherd's neck and chest combines with round, wide-set eyes and triangular, high-set ears to give this herding dog a playful look!

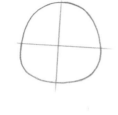
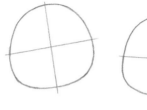

1

2

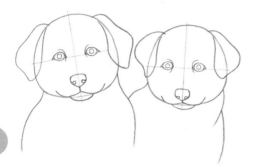

3

4

5